SHANNON POSHE ANDERSON

THE
GLOW
UP

YOUR 30 DAY PLAYBOOK TO GLOWING UP,
SHOWING UP, AND GETTING
WHAT YOU WANT

This book has been printed in the United States of America 2020
ISBN: 978-0-578-71968-9

Power Of Purpose Publishing
3355 Lenox Rd
Atlanta, Ga 30326
www.PopPublishing.com
www.LoveAndLiveYourMessage.com

THE
GLOW
UP

Get My Free Training

Ready to write and publish your book?

Go to www.WriteAndPublishIn90Days.com

Dedication

I would like to dedicate this book to you, the reader. The person who's looking for change. The person who's ready to stop playing small and start showing up BIG. The person who's tried everything else and at last is ready to do the work. I call forth all of the dreamers, wishers, and believers who are seeking to know the steps to living a happier life. I call forth the new and improved version of YOU. The person who's now "On Glow."

Table of Contents

Prologue

The term "Glow Up" is a term widely used in today's society. Yet, depending on who you ask it may have many meanings. Some believe in a physical glow up. A glow up that is seen externally by everyone, such as a weight loss, new hairdo, or makeover.

There are also financial glow ups where you are able to upgrade your financial situation to one that meets your needs and wants. There are personal glow ups and these are glow ups of personal transformation. A change on how a person sees the world, has a better outlook on life and themselves, and in turn lives a happy and healthier life. What if you could do all of these things?

I mean what if you were able to glow up in every area of your life? What if you were able to reach a total transformation in your personal life, physical, and financial life? Well, this is what this book is for. Glowing up and touching on every area of your life. This book will give you tips and tricks on increasing self awareness, self healing, weight loss and nutrition, as well as financial tips. Now I am not saying that this book is the answer to everything. Life is all about learning from now and until we leave this earth. However, I've created an easy to read book that will get you started on the right path and in turn provide the starting place.

Finally a book that will give you tips and touch on every aspect of your life, this is the Glow UP!

Have you fallen down and had to get back up again? My guess is yes, but have you really fallen down? I mean to the point of despair? To the point of brokenness?

Feeling so weak that even when you tried to get up your knees would buckle under the pressure, If you haven't fallen down in this way then no worries!

The Glow up is for those individuals who have felt like they wanted to give up, whose backs were against the wall and who have felt as if they would never make it.

The person who has been talked about, left out, counted out, time and time again. Those who have a burning desire to succeed but just now sure how. Those who are feeling stuck and unproductive who just need that extra push and that extra support. You know that there is something deep down on the inside that is better than where you are.

You know that God has placed something deep down inside of you that is yearning to get out. Well, let me tell you, I know that feeling all too well. My name is Shannon Poshe Anderson and I am an author, speaker, publisher, certified life/business coach, and survivor.

I can relate to this story on so many levels. I grew up in an abusive household with an alcoholic father. To say that my household was unstable is an understatement. I then was sexually abused at the age of 11 by my sister's boyfriend and this led me down the wrong track and led to a chain of events that severely affected my self esteem and self worth.

I eventually ended up stripping in clubs by the age of 15 and the cycle of self abuse and self betrayal continued on many years after that. Then finally in 2015, I wrote my first book " Stripper To Striver" after being involved in a fatal car crash that killed my manager and left me traumatized and broken once again. However, this was the very turning point that I needed to set myself on the right track.

A great shift had taken place, the old me died and a new me emerged. I decided on that fateful day of March 24th, 2015 that I would change my life forever, no matter what the cost, and no matter how long it took.

I knew that my life had been spared for a reason and I wanted to see the full manifestation of what life had for me. Is this you?

Intro

Now, unbelievably this is not the place where the " Glow Up" happened for me. I did release the book, I did do some of the work, however the breakthrough did not happen here. I know what you're thinking, then when did it come?

Here is an excerpt from my journal that I wrote on my birthday, July 22nd, 2017, as I was sitting in my hospital bed. I had just been robbed, drug in a car, and had my arm broken. Yes, Another tragedy.

"As I sit here on another birthday, I am sitting here in yet another transitional place. One of brokenness, shame, and defeat. Yet with another glimpse I can see that it's not defeat at all but another tipping point on the scale that's meant to be pushed. My scale should have been heavier, I should have added more baggage so that I could be pushed out of my comfort zone.

I came to play, yet I came to play it safe, and in turn cost me to lose yet once again. I should have served more and given even more. I now stand in my naked truth, my truth of unwillingness to give until it hurt. My truth of wanting to get in the game then sit on the sidelines because I didn't want to get hurt.

My truth of not properly serving the people that GOD had intended me to serve. My truth of not allowing for his grace and message to flow through me, so that it would impact and change lives at a much higher capacity because I refused to be stretched to the point of unrecognition.

4

Admitting to the truth that I was paralyzed by my fear of not wanting to be judged or ridiculed. My truth of failing myself yet once again.

Now, the "Glow Up" begins

Phase 1

HEAL THYSELF

Heal Thyself

Healing yourself is by far the hardest and longest portion of the glow up. Healing is a process that cannot and should not be rushed. It is through your healing process that you will uncover a number of things.

The most important thing that you will discover is who you are at your core. During this process you will have to unravel everything that has tied you in bondage. It is a painful, yet humbling process. However, in order to reach the "full" glow up it cannot be skipped.

You are not glowing if you are not healed. If you do not endure the healing process you are doomed to end up back in the same place that you were before or worse. Not healing properly allows you to skip digging deep and pinpointing the things that led you there to begin with. I know it may be uncomfortable, however nothing worth having really is.

The things that we want the most will require us to grow the most. I will try to make this as interesting and as fun as I can make it. Trust me it will be more than worth it, you owe it to yourself!

Get Naked...Remove the Mask

Throughout the following year I had to really get naked with myself. I had to really pull back the curtain and allow myself to see who I truly was. What I realized was that I was a lot more broken than what I had seen before.

I realized that there were still shadows lurking behind those curtains that I wasn't proud of. I realized that all of the hurt and shame that I had experienced throughout my life was still there. I realized that I wasn't as healed as I thought that I was and the woman that I was portraying to be had not arrived yet. OUCH!

Yes that stung, however I knew that if I were to be the woman that GOD truly called me to be, I had to get real. I had to come clean with myself because no one else could do that for me. Yes it hurt, it hurt a lot! But ask yourself, are you willing to hurt temporarily to get through to your breakthrough, or are you willing to hurt for a lifetime? I was tired of hurting, so I took matters into my own hands. I had to get naked and remove all masks!

Now I know what you're thinking, get naked, really? No, yes, I mean no, not really. Getting naked simply means getting real with yourself. Yes, cutting out the nonsense and digging deep and getting to the root of the problem. What are those things that are bothering you? What are those deep down secrets that you have hidden from the rest of the world that keeps you in bondage? What are those thoughts, actions, or relationships that you are ashamed to admit, yet you bury them deep down inside of you only to rot and eat away at you little by little?

Yes, these deep dark secrets eat away at you from the inside out and before you know it they build up into these huge mountains that are plaguing you daily.So here are a set of questions that you can ask yourself.

What does your dream life look like?

_____

_____

_____

_____

_____

What are the main things that you feel have kept you from achieving this life?

_____

_____

_____

_____

_____

Action Steps:

Get a journal and designate it as your healing journal. Write down what your dream life looks like, see it and imagine it in your mind. Feel the feelings as if you already have it. Now write down the things that you feel are keeping you from attaining this life.

We are all more aware of our barriers more than we would like to admit. It is usually our thoughts, actions, and relationships that keep us from attaining our dream lives. Remember Get Real with yourself!

Write down a list of things that you can do to change these situations.

What thoughts, feelings, and people are holding you back?

_____

_____

_____

_____

Who are the people or situations that you will need in order to receive your ultimate healing? Ex. Spiritual Counselor or healer, Minister, Confidant, Mentor, Coach, Good listener, Healing Retreat, etc...

_____

_____

_____

_____

_____

Who are the people that you need to remove?

_____

_____

_____

_____

_____

Do your due diligence by researching and reaching out to the people or situations mentioned in number 3 who you think you need most.

P.S. Keep in mind that through your healing process you may need to isolate yourself from others and the things that are tearing you down.

This is crucial in this process. Please take heed. You cannot do the same things and expect a different outcome. There will be change in this season.

"Everything that you could ever want is on the other side of your comfort zone"

Step Out of Your Comfort Zone

Now I mentioned before about being in a comfort zone. I know this all too well. Your comfort zone is what I call the tight cocoon of mediocrity. It squeezes you so tightly that it's hard to reach beyond where you currently are. However, I promise you. If you can see it, you can achieve it.

I could remember having all of these grand dreams. I could see it all so well. The house I would live in, the car I would drive, the husband, the career, and the kids. It was so bright yet the path to get there was so unclear. I mean how could I accomplish all of these things? Just thinking about it made me feel exhausted, overwhelmed, scared, alone, and confused.

Then there was the negative self talk that came soon after. " You can't do that?" "What if they laugh at you?" " What if no one believes you?" " Who's gonna listen to you?"

Then before you know it, there I was shrinking back into the tight cocoon again. Even though it was holding me back, it felt safe and familiar. Sound familiar? The overwhelm of feeling insignificant would come and choke the life out of my very dreams. It would take me back to when I had just been molested by my sister's boyfriend.

I was 11 years old and felt lost, confused, afraid, and alone. I would reach out to my family to tell them but no one believed me. In fact I was blamed for it.

This caused so much mistrust and confusion in my life. It taught me that no one would believe me and that my voice didn't matter. It was ultimately one of the many scars that would keep me from truly pursuing my dreams.

What are some of your scars?

_____

_____

_____

_____

What are some of the negative things that you have been telling yourself?

_____

_____

_____

_____

_____

What experiences happened in your life that could have caused the negative self talk and self doubt?

_____

_____

_____

_____

_____

Receive Divine Guidance & Pray

The next step into seeking your ultimate " glow up" is to receive divine guidance from your creator. Some may refer to this as GOD or some may refer to it as the universe, whatever your preference make sure that you receive divine guidance and connection from your source.

Praying and asking for guidance from GOD has been a life changer for me! If it were not for that I don't know where I would be. I make it my business to pray and ask for guidance daily.

Action Steps:

1.Every morning before you rise, take 15-30 minutes to seek your creator through prayer and or meditation. Ask for their guidance. Ask questions to seek your divine purpose.

2. Buy a journal specifically designated for this. Once you hear direction and guidance, use this journal to write down what your source is telling you. Keep track, listen, and follow directions.

Affirm

The next step in the process is the affirmation process.

Here you will scour the internet, bible, or whatever source that you can find and seek out positive quotes, affirmations, or scriptures that you can repeat to yourself over and over again throughout the day.

For example whenever I am feeling weak, one of my favorite affirmations is " I can achieve ALL things through Jesus Christ who strengthens me." I repeat this scripture more than any other because it is the one that I need most.

Take some time to find things that will motivate and inspire you. REPEAT and read ALOUD everyday. For better results look in the mirror everyday and read them to yourself while looking at yourself. Place sticky notes throughout the areas that you visit the most and have these quotes written on them to motivate you throughout the day.

What are your quotes, affirmations, or scriptures?

1. _____

   _____

2. _____

   _____

3. _____

   _____

4. _____

_____

5. _____

_____

P.S Read one positive thing and listen to one positive message daily. This will help to retrain your subconscious mind. You can read books, articles, or blogs. You can listen to things online such as video's or podcasts to continuously feed your mind and spirit positive messages. Do this at least 2 times daily.

"Your new life is awaiting you.
It's all up to you"

All It Takes Is A Mustard Seed...

Now there were several times that I had to release my faith. In the beginning it was truly scary. I had very little faith. Even though I knew that GOD had been there for me countless times, it was still hard for me to let go and to trust. I remember when I was on the run from my husband. I had left him because of all of the domestic abuse that was going on.

I depended on him financially at the time and was terrified about stepping out on my own. However, I knew that there wasn't a choice now. The police had carried him away and he was not able to return to the home. I had to trust and believe that things would work out and that things would be ok.

Ultimately I ended up being in a better position than I was before I left him. I was able to get back on my feet and provide for my kids. It gave me the confidence to go out and start businesses and accomplish other things in my life.

GOD said that all you need is a mustard seed of faith. That's a very small amount. Thank GOD for that! I could at least do that right? Can you believe in a mustard seed of faith? I promise that if you do you will see significant change in your life.

Faith is one of the major keys throughout your glow up process. Believing that you already have it is crucial. The more that you believe, the faster things will start to happen for you. The bible says " Seek and ye shall find"

The more that you release your faith and " seek" the more you shall find.

What is something that you can do today to walk in faith?

_____

_____

_____

_____

_____

What are you believing for in your life?

_____

_____

_____

_____

_____

"You don't need to see the whole staircase. Just take the first step"
~Martin Luther King

Forgive/Level Up

Now here is one of the most difficult processes of the glow up and that is forgiveness. Now, this step will take you into parts of yourself that require you to be humble and vulnerable. This is the step that keeps the most people in bondage. Why? I believe for several reasons. It requires you to not only get, real but to address the matter at hand. It may also cause you to confront people or situations you may not be ready to address.

As humans, most of us can acknowledge a situation, but addressing it is something completely different. It's so much easier to just sweep things under the rug than it is to address things head on. However, I assure you that forgiveness is the process that will set you free the most.

I remember a few weeks after the car accident that took the life of my manager and almost took mine as well. My father who I had been estranged from for several years offered to take me to lunch. At this meeting my father apologized for not being there and stated that he wished that he had done more.

I had been asking my father to own up to his mistakes for years. I would always get the same story. Oh I didn't know that I left you guys homeless. After he had left us and then remarried another woman and didn't look back. Or, I didn't know that my drinking and abusive behavior caused so much torment in your life. All of which I knew was a bunch of crap. Deep down he knew it too.

Which is why after seeing that he could have lost me, did he apologize. I was 37 years old and felt like I had been waiting my whole life to hear this. I forgave him. I felt free.

P.S Remember that forgiveness is not for the other person. It's really for us

Name the people or person whom you need to forgive the most?

P.S One of these people may even be you. Yes, you may need to forgive yourself.

_____

_____

_____

_____

_____

Name the thing or things that you or others have done to betray you? Yes, it is possible to betray yourself. Name those things too

_____

_____

_____

_____

_____

Who do you need to forgive?

_____

_____

_____

_____

_____

Who do you need to apologize to?

_____

_____

_____

_____

_____

Forgive those who have done you wrong. If you can, reach out and let them know that you have forgiven them. Also, reach out to those who need to forgive you and ask for forgiveness.

Congratulations, you have released a huge amount of bondage!

Phase 2
Love THYSELF

Celebrate Yourself

Now that we are unraveling, getting real, forgiving, affirming, and creating new processes it is now time to renew our strength. This can be an exhausting process so we deserve a fun day! Reach out to your favorite people and plan an outing with them. Do something fun and celebrate yourself. Let your trusted loved ones know about your new journey, allow them to encourage you and celebrate you as well.

P.S This outing must be made with people who truly support you. No nay sayers or negative people are allowed on this outing. It doesn't matter how much you love them. If they do not truly support you they are not allowed.

Self Care

Take some time to do some self care. Self care is necessary for the glow up. We must look and feel good. There is only one you and you deserve to have some pampering! What can you do to spoil or pamper yourself today? Ex,, Hot bath, massage, reading, makeover, or quick getaway. Let's go!

_____

_____

_____

_____

_____

*"You're about to go into a
season where you are about to receive
breakthrough after breakthrough
because you didn't allow it to break you!"*

Accountability/Teamwork

If you haven't done so already, link with someone whom

you can trust who will hold you accountable for completing tasks. This could be someone from the group of people that you selected on your outing, or someone like a counselor or a therapist. Either way, it is very smart to have a person or people who will motivate you and keep you on track . Grab a friend or two and glow up together! Go to www.IamShannonAnderson.com and grab another copy of this book for them too. It's always better with a group!

Name Your Accountability Partners

_____

_____

_____

_____

_____

Lead with love

Approach everyone and every situation in love. If you are not at a place where you can then don't approach it at all. If you don't have something nice to say about a situation politely let the person know that you choose not to respond or be involved, this keeps negative energy from coming back to you. It's okay to give constructive criticism as long it's done in love.

However, if you are giving out advice solely based on tearing someone else down. Beware, it WILL return to you. You've been warned.

I remember when I had to truly start walking in love. I had been hurt so much in my life, and I had spent many years returning the favor. Hurt people hurt people and I was at war! If you had a problem with me I had a problem with you. If you were coming for me I was surely coming for you!

What I found over the years is that we attract what we put out. Once I understood how the laws of attraction work (you should really watch the movie Laws Of Attraction) then everything started to make so much sense to me.

Once I started putting out positive energy, positive energy flowed back to me. So try as much as you can to put out positive energy. Take a deep breath and let it flow. You'll thank me later. ;)

"Give and it shall be given unto you; good measure, pressed down, and shaken together, and running over, shall men give into your bosom."

Luke 6:38

Develop An "I Win" Persona

Believe that you deserve all of the good things that are coming your way. Now I know what you're thinking. Of course I believe that I deserve the best. Do you really?

I cannot tell you how many times my clients have said that they deserved the best, then when the things that they have been trying to manifest start to appear, they start to shut down and sabotage the very things that they have been praying for and working for.

If you think about it carefully, I am sure that you have done the same thing

at some point in your life. Once that job appeared you ran, once that relationship appeared you sabotaged it because you thought that it was too good to be true. Now in this exercise, we are going to pinpoint those things that we have sabotaged because we did not believe that we deserved them at our core.

All of this is linked to a real hindrance called self destructive behavior. Self destruction is usually tied to our self worth. Believing that you are worthy in your mind is one thing, believing it in your heart is another.

Once I developed an "I Win" Persona I was able to take on the world in a new way. Believing in my heart that I will win any situation that I'm in helped me to create the life that I truly wanted.

Speaking my affirmations daily, meditating, praying, and visualizing all helped me to do this.

What practices can you use to develop your I Win Persona?

1. Write a list of the things that you believe you have sabotaged?

_____

_____

_____

_____

_____

2. Why do you believe that you sabotaged these things?

_____

_____

_____

_____

_____

3. What are some things that you can do differently to prevent this from happening again?

_____

_____

_____

_____

_____

4. What event or events happened in your past that would have affected your self esteem and self worth?

_____

_____

_____

_____

5. Does this person or situation need to be forgiven? Do you need to be forgiven because of something that you did to cause this situation? Write it out

_____

_____

_____

_____

_____

6. Write out some affirmations and soul work that you can do to walk you into truly believing that you deserve the very best.

_____

_____

_____

_____

_____

P.S I have included an affirmation on the next page.

"I am the best
I deserve the best
Because I give my best
Only good things can come to me"

Do your very best...
Have patience with yourself

Always aim to do and give your very best in any situation. This behavior will challenge you and cause you to grow continuously. Getting complacent is the enemy of growth and progress, so always make it your business to give your best to others and situations. You will then find that others will also do the same for you. Once again, everything that we put out is always what we will receive back.

Be patient with yourself. These things take time. Commit to giving your best daily. Start slow them progress from there. Forgive yourself often. Make a note of when you mess up, tell yourself that it's ok and that you are learning and growing. Take a note of your triggers and what makes you revert back, then try not to place yourself in those positions if possible. If you have to be in certain situations, or around certain people that trigger you; such as in a job then approach the situation differently. Practice seeing it in a more positive light so that you can deal with it more appropriately.

Here is my patience message that I say every-time that I mess up and revert to an old habit. "It's ok Shannon, you're getting better everyday. You are learning and growing, it's ok."

What positive message can you tell yourself when you feel that you have messed up or reverted back to an old habit?

_____

_____

_____

_____

_____

Know that you will be tested.

Just like in anything else that you learn ,you will be tested. However once you know this walking in you will be ready for whatever comes your way. Once you see the test, PASS it or you will be doomed to keep repeating it. That is one of the biggest keys in life. Want to know why you keep going through the same thing over and over again? It's because you did not pass the test.

Learn to identify tests when they occur, once you pass it then you can move on to the next level. Stop allowing the same people to upset you. Stop falling for the same tricks over and over again and you will see, a new door will be opened to you.

I personally stay quiet for a minute and think about what response I will give. I no longer move out of impulse. Impulsive behavior is dangerous!

I think about my response, sometimes my response could be just to walk away. It's still a response, yet a response that is likely to work in my favor by avoiding possible pitfalls.

What can you do to prepare yourself for the test?

_____

_____

_____

_____

_____

How will you handle situations that test you?

_____

_____

_____

_____

_____

Don't Compare Yourself....
You're Great!

The journey is real. That is the most important thing that I can say about comparison. So what exactly does that mean? Well, it simply means that you cannot compare your journey to someone else's.

You have no idea what sacrifices that they made to be in the position that they're in. How many long nights, overdrawn bank accounts, and how many friends they may have lost along the way.

Moral of the story is this, be patient with yourself. Enjoy YOUR journey because it is yours. No one else will walk the exact same path as you and you won't walk the same path as someone else. We may have similar destinations but I guarantee the journey to get there will be different. Embrace it, own it, and learn along the way.

"Comparison is the thief of all joy"

Don't sweat the small stuff

It is highly important to not sweat the small stuff. Stressing out over things is not only unhealthy it also causes us to become unproductive. Not everything deserves your response or attention. Some things are better left alone. Did you know that stress is a major factor in many illnesses today? From heart disease, cancer, ulcers and more. Stress plagues your body and literally causes you to break down from the inside out. So do yourself a favor and choose your battles wisely.

What are some habits, situations, or people that have caused you to become stressed?

_____

_____

_____

_____

What are some things that you can do to destress several times weekly?
(Ex: Walks, Massages, Watch funny movies, hot bubble baths, exercise)

_____

_____

_____

_____

Phase 3
Build Thyself

Get Fit

What if I told you that having a healthy diet and exercise regimen could prolong your life and improve your way of living? Of course you know that. However, it is astonishing to me how many people choose not to follow it. Start small then work your way up gradually.

Try replacing soda with water a few times per week. Instead of eating a burger, substitute it for a salad also a few times a week. Park farther away from the door of your destination to get more steps added to your day. Instead of taking the elevator try taking the stairs once a day.

Instead of eating cereals and foods that are high in calories and sugars, try juicing for breakfast instead. Trying a few of these tactics and then increasing them slowly over time will get you on the path of living a healthier life. What can you do today to give you your jump start?

Get my glow up kit!

TheGlowUpBook.com

What steps can you take to get you off to living a healthier life?

_____

_____

_____

_____

_____

_____

What are you looking to improve in terms of health and fitness?

_____

_____

_____

_____

_____

_____

What has held you back from achieving this goal so far?

_____

_____

_____

_____

_____

What can you do differently to keep you on track to attaining your health and fitness goals?

_____

_____

_____

_____

_____

_____

P.S Remember to take your vitamins and supplements. Go to www.IamShannonAnderson.com to get more info on how to live a healthier and happier life

Boss Up Your Credit

Now one thing that I have learned is that bad credit ain't cute. I sure am a witness to that. I dealt with bad credit for years. Messing up my credit in my early 20's was a huge mistake and something that I had to deal with the effects of for many years.

Unfortunately, many of us did not have the privilege of having parents who taught us about the effects of having bad credit. Many of us had to learn it the hard way and spend many years frustrated and overwhelmed with debt.

Many of our parents were also struggling with their own credit and debt issues, therefore not being able to teach us properly. However I have learned a few tips along the way that I have personally used to place myself in the 700 club.

1. The first step to bossing up your credit is to pull your credit file. You can do this annually for free at www. annualcreditreport.Com

2. Look over all of your accounts and identify which ones are inaccurate or incorrect.

3. Dispute all inaccuracies and incorrect reporting. The best way to do this is to use dispute letters and send them certified mail to the creditor letting them know that they are being disputed. Log onto www.creditlikeaboss.com for more tips on how to get hold of dispute letters in my Credit Like A Boss ebook and guide.

4. If the creditor does not respond, write a letter to each credit bureau, TransUnion, Equifax, and Experian letting them know that the creditor did not respond within the 30 day time period. (Check the time frame for your state) In the letter place the mailing confirmation number from the certified mail letter that you sent.

5. By law the credit bureaus have to remove any items that the creditor does not respond to.

6. If the creditor does respond with an itemized bill, write the creditor back letting them know that an itemized bill is not a legally binding contract and cannot be used as a way of proving a debt owed to them and that they need to send something with your signature and legally binding. This is letter no 2 in my credit like a boss ebook.

7. Send a letter to the credit bureau letting them know that the creditor is violating your rights by sending an itemized bill and that they are obligated to remove the item by law.

Credit booster tip:

If you have a credit card or any card that is in good standing, Call and ask for a credit line increase. This will automatically lower your utilization rate and increase your credit score without having to do anything.

Do not use the new amount that has been given to you. Instead continue to pay down your balance and watch your credit score rise!

What accounts are you disputing?

_____

_____

_____

Dates of disputes:

_____

_____

_____

Dates & Response of disputes: (Verified, Deleted, Etc)

_____

_____

_____

Confirmation Numbers of certified mail:

_____

_____

_____

Go to www.annualcreditreport .com and pull all 3 bureaus. Download the reports to your computer. You can even dispute from the website as well.

Need more help? Get my ebook filled with more tips and dispute letters and credit boosting tips that you can use. Go to www.CreditLikeABoss.com to get your copy.

Get Aligned & Get What You Want

I can't tell you how many times I have felt stuck and didn't know how to push forward. Here are a few tips that I used to catapult my life into the right direction.

1. Detox and Purge

Detox and cleanse any negative energy or bad vibes. This could be from people that you associate with or hang around, places that you go, or activities that you participate in. Think of the things and people who drain your energy and cause you to get off track. These are clear indications that these are people and situations that you need to remove yourself from. Take a moment and think of these people and situations and write them down.

1.   *I am purging*

_____

_____

_____

_____

_____

2.   *Get aligned*

Get aligned with your higher self. Practice meditation, pray daily, and take time to listen to what it is that GOD and the universe is telling you. Make sure that you take time daily to get into a quiet space so that you can hear. Write down the things that GOD and the universe are directing you to do

Prayer and Meditation are the best ways to get aligned.

- Prayer

  Praying to your GOD or a source higher than you to me is the best way to align. I like to pray first thing in the morning and also read my bible before bed. This helps me to feel strong, connected, and peaceful

- Meditation

  Meditation is another powerful way to align. Some people swear by this and practice meditation daily. Get into a quiet comfortable space on the floor or on a chair. Clear your mind and focus on your breaths. The goal is to find a place of calm and peace. A great app for beginners to use is called Headspace. Download the app and get started today! It will walk you through step by step.

- Reiki

  Reiki is a form of energy healing. It is a Japanese technique for stress deduction and healing. I am actually a licensed Reiki practitioner. I give myself Reiki daily and it has truly helped to heal me. I am also able to give it to other people. Reiki is also referred to as Chakra balancing. Shifting the energy in the body and balancing out the Chakras is truly life changing!

- *Acupuncture*

  Acupuncture is a Chinese practice that is also widely used. While I have never practiced it myself I have read that it is very useful in reducing stress.

- *Aroma Therapy*

  Aromatherapy is a holistic healing treatment that uses aromatic essential oils medicinally to improve the health of the body, mind, and spirit. What ways will you use to align?

When will you get started?

_____

_____

_____

_____

_____

_____

What is it that GOD and the universe are directing you to do?

_____

_____

_____

_____

_____

Unplug

Unplug yourself from all of the noise that is happening daily. This could be from media, such as tv and radio, social media, youtube, and other channels that are feeding you information continuously. Be careful as to what vices you are allowing to feed you information. These things can be toxic and detrimental.

What are those people and situations that drain you or distract you from your purpose and goals?

_____

_____

_____

_____

_____

_____

Fill up on the good things

Now that you are detoxing and unplugging, it is time for you to fill up on the good things. Good books, interviews, podcasts, and media that feed your soul and your interests. Get more knowledgeable on the things that GOD and the universe have instructed you to do. For instance if they are telling you to become a hairstylist, get more education on that, go to school, learn more things in that field. The more you know the more you earn.

What are the books, people , and sources that cause me to feel good and reach my goals?

_____

_____

_____

_____

_____

_____

Take Action

'Now that you have gotten the information. Do not sit on it. Use the information as soon as you can. Whenever you learn something new you should put it to use within 24-48 hours. The universe responds to speed. Have faith that things will work out in your favor.

Use these and GET UNSTUCK today!!! I promise you it will be worth it, take your energy and activate change.

Serenity is vital to success

As I said previously, Stress causes so many problems in the human body, it causes a strain and oftentimes it leads to depression. It's best to practice resourceful habits and healthy living so that when stressful situations arise, you deal with them without becoming overwhelmed. I know the battles of depression.

I was diagnosed with depression at the age of 8. By the time I was 11 I had had a breakdown and was hospitalized in a mental facility until the age of 12. Due to the overwhelming stress and things that I was experiencing in my home I was diagnosed with depression, anxiety, and PTSD.

Some healthy habits that you can adapt to obtain from stress is waking up early, meditation, eating breakfast and taking your vitamins. Healthy and clean eating habits, exercise, and going to sleep early are also great ways to reduce stress. These steps are vital to your success, they bring serenity into your life and fill your spirit with peacefulness. Waking up early allows you to rise before the busy hours begin, you can watch the sunrise and it will help you to begin your day without rushing off to work.

Meditating or reading something inspirational in the morning when you wake will place peace into your morning and help you start your day off right. You can enjoy a cup of tea, hot water with lemon or coffee at this time as well. Eating breakfast and taking your vitamins are vital to your health.

They give you the energy that you need and fill your belly up with nutrients in the morning. Practicing healthy and clean eating habits will not only make you healthy but give you energy. Exercising is essential to success, it gives you balance and increases good health. Lastly, going to bed early allows you to have enough sleep to wake up early. It allows your mind to be at ease and let go of the stressors of the day.

Serenity is vital to your success and practicing these steps will help give you more peace and happiness in your life. They say it takes 21 days to form a habit, take these steps that I have given to you and apply them to your life. You will be sure to be successful and peaceful throughout your life.

Tip: Use smudge sticks (sage) to burn around your home and office. This will clear out and absorb negative energy and clear the path for positive energy to flow in.

Glow Up In 3 Easy Steps

Ok so the glow up is oh so real! I can remember feeling hopeless, stuck, overwhelmed, and confused on my journey. I remember feeling as if I would never get to where I was supposed to be. Trust me, the tips in this book are tips that I used personally to elevate my life. These next 3 tips are vital ones to me.

The "glow up" tips as I call them definitely helped me to get to where I am today. My clients have found the tips in this book just as useful and the next 3 very pertinent. While they may seem obvious, it is actually putting them into action, that is where the reward is.

3 Vital Steps To Consider

1. Increase your faith. Increasing your faith is crucial for attaining the life that you dream about. You have to first believe that you can achieve it before you will ever see it. One thing that I did and still do consistently is to pray and to get answers from GOD or from your higher source.

   No one can give you direction better than that. Once you have done that, believe that what was told to you is true and live as though it is already yours.

2. Stop second guessing yourself. Yes! You are fabulous. You are beautifully and wonderfully made and there is no one who can do it like you. So stop second guessing yourself and use your gifts to bless the world.

3. Take action. OMG! Please take action, stop sleeping on your plans and gifts. You are going to have to put some work behind that plan. Your plans won't work themselves. Set small attainable goals that lead to your major goal. A little work a day goes a long way.

Take A Chance On Yourself

Take a chance on yourself! Play big and not small. Aspire to do great things and actually believe that you can. Set gigantic goals. Goals so big that scare you.

Yes, this is where the faith comes in. Move forward as if it's already done and watch how God and the universe will align things for you. Also, even if you fall short, wouldn't you rather fall short of a gigantic goal versus a small one?

If you want to take gigantic steps in your life.

Read the book 10x by Grant Cardone.

Name that dream that is so big that it scares you

_____

_____

_____

_____

What is one HUGE step that you can take today that will help move your dream forward?

_____

_____

_____

_____

"Never reduce the target. Increase the action"

~Grant Cardone

Standout! Be A Flamingo In
A Flock of Pigeons

Ok Ok now I know that some may think that this is harsh, but it's really not. In order to take things to the next level you're going to have to elevate and rise like a shining star in the midnight sky. You will not be able to be like everyone else.

You can't be amongst the flock and change the world at the same time. You are going to have to be different. So this saying holds true. Morph into the beautiful butterfly that GOD says that you are. Transform into the breathtaking flamingo. Stand out. Be Seen. Change The World.

What can you do to stand out and be true to you?

Ex dye your hair, express your thoughts openly, do that thing that you have been too afraid to do!

_____

_____

_____

_____

_____

_____

"You can't be amongst the flock and change the world at the same time"
~Shannon Poshe Anderson

Isolation Is Required for Elevation

Now in order to glow up and become our best selves GOD will use isolation to do this. There will be a period when you will have to isolate yourself and be in relationship with GOD and the universe to get your instructions. Remember, only one person has the blueprint to your purpose. Seek him and follow the plan.

Get a journal specifically for hearing from GOD, As you are following the steps, you are detoxing and should be hearing from GOD more clearly. Write down what he is saying. Pay attention to what he is doing. Write everything down, pay attention, and follow instructions.

The Power of Visualization/Creation

I remember setting goals and wanting to achieve them. I would write them down and then leave them in a journal. It wasn't until I learned about visualization that things started to change for me. I once watched a young lady whip out her whiteboard, glue sticks, glitter, and magazines and got to work.

I was in awe as I watched her carefully place each strip of paper that she had cut out from a magazine onto her board. She deliberately and carefully placed each picture down and spoke that these were the visions that she had seen for herself. These were the goals that she was setting out to accomplish and now they became more real to her because she was able to see them. Now I have to admit, I wasn't sold the first time that I saw this, however I did think that it was "cute."

It wasn't until I started to see the wave of vision boards popping up all over social media that I decided to do a little bit more investigating. After my research, I found that indeed vision boards were not just some cute arts and crafts project, (which is what I proclaimed it to be. lol.) But that it was something that people were swearing by and believed worked into obtaining the things that they wanted.

So I decided to try it for myself, I went on a store run, bought every magazine that appealed to me, glue, boards, and any other cute knick knacks that inspired me from the arts and crafts section of the store, went home and went to work. I then hung it on my wall.

Looked at it every morning and everynight and sometimes throughout the day.

Then I would stare at it and envision myself in that home, that car, or on Oprah's couch lol. Before long some of those things began to manifest. Now I wanted to learn more of HOW this stuff even works. So I then began to do more research.

What I found out was something that I had already known. The things that we focus on the most, are the things that manifest in our lives. The good old Law of Attraction at work but now thanks to the vision board it was now working on steroids. Once we can see it we can be it!

So take some time and scour the internet, get magazines of your favorite places, cars, and anything that you want to manifest. Print or cut them out and place them on boards in your journal or place on your wall.Look at them multiple times a day and see yourself actually owning them. The key is to FEEL the experience.

Try making your vision board today and see how it improves your life.

In order to go where you want to go, you have to be able to see it. The power of visualization is a powerful tool to use. Take out time preferably in the morning before you get out of bed, close your eyes and envision your dreams and your life goals. Tell yourself that you can do it over and over again. Repeat your affirmations daily, pray over the vision, and see yourself actually living out your dream in vivid detail. Create a vision board if necessary and look at it everyday.

P.S. Remember to FEEL it!

Go to www.IamShannonAnderson.com to get more info about me

Build A Bankable Business

A huge glow up for me came when I was able to start and run my business successfully. Nothing beats being able to provide for yourself and your family while doing what you love!

So I have provided some great tips for you to be able to launch a business and live a life on your terms!

1. Determine the Name Of Your Brand. Find a name that is catchy and unique. Try to stay away from names that are common and already used.

2. Secure Your Name On All Social Media Platforms. Secure Your Name On Every Social Media Outlet such as Instagram, Pinterest, Facebook, etc.

3. Register Your Web Address. When you're ready to register your domain you can go to Godaddy.com, Domain.com. Even Shopify.com, and Wordpress.com will allow you to register your domain name. (Godaddy is the best)

4. Get a website. There are several companies that you can use to host your site. You have Shopify.com, Wix.com, Squarespace.com, Godaddy.com ,and Big Cartel.com just to name a few. Try out their free trials and ultimately select your favorite host.

Have a Positive Mindset

Having a Positive mindset is the first thing that you need to succeed. Without it, it will be very hard to sustain in your business. Keep a list of positive affirmations that you can say everyday.

I have included a few at the end of this that you can continue to say to yourself everyday. Keep a group of positive people around you as much as you can. Stay clear of negativity and naysayers as much as possible.

Stay around people who inspire you and who want to see you succeed. Look up inspirational icons and get inspiration from them.

Do Something that sets Your heart on fire! Are you working on your gift and your purpose?

I ask this because business will not always be easy and sometimes you will have to lean on the fact that you are walking in your true passion and gift to sustain you during the hard times

Doing what sets your heart on fire will get you through the tough times. Here are some tips that you can use to help to try to get you there.

What is it that you love to do more than anything in the world?

_____

_____

_____

_____

_____

What is that something that you could do and not get paid for?

_____

_____

_____

_____

How can you monetize it?

_____

_____

_____

_____

How much time and money are you willing to invest in your business? Write out a paragraph detailing how much you really believe in yourself & your business.

Believing in your business and brand is crucial to your survival and success. Write out an affirmation for your business. ex.I believe in myself and my business. I believe that I have everything that it takes to thrive!

_____

_____

_____

_____

_____

_____

Are you telling the whole world about your business or are you only letting a select amount of people know?

Are you willing to invest in your business every week.? Ex. I am willing to invest 30 minutes per day into my business. I have an additional 100.00 per week that I can utilize towards marketing my business or educating myself in my business.

Am I prepared to market and speak up for my business everyday? What are 3 things that you can start doing in your business tomorrow to get the word out about it?

_____

_____

_____

_____

_____

_____

Research

Doing research in your business will prove to serve you well for the long haul. It is very important to know the current trends of your business. Also, it is very important to know who your competitors are and what they're doing.

It's also important to know who your collaborators are. Make a list of your Competitors & Collaborators (Collaborators are Companies that compliment your brand that you can work with)

Name Competitors

_____

_____

_____

_____

_____

_____

What collaborators can you reach out to that can help to grow your brand Now reach out to them!

Budget

Having a budget is a critical part of your business. Knowing how much money you have to work with can keep you from drowning before you even get off to a good start.

There are several things that you will need to budget for, here are a few. You can google good budgeting and Marketing Plans: How much money do you have for marketing your business per month?

_____

_____

_____

_____

_____

_____

Expenses

What is the total cost to run your business every month? Include products and the cost of operating expenses such as website, rent, utilities, etc...

Planning

Now you will need to create a good marketing and business plan. I won't go too deep into plans because they can get quite extensive, however answering these questions will get you off to a great start. Who is my target? List 5 characteristics of the people that you will be marketing to. ex. Age, Sex, Hobbies, Career, etc

How will you market to your ideal client?

_____

_____

_____

_____

_____

Where will you market to your ideal client? Ex. Instagram Ads

_____

_____

_____

_____

_____

How often will you market to your ideal client?

_____

_____

_____

_____

_____

List your Top 5 goals of what you would like to accomplish in your business. Give yourself a date and a time limit to finish by.

_____

_____

_____

_____

_____

Mentorship

Having a good mentor or coach will help speed along the process greatly of running a business. Being able to get someone's expertise and advice is always a great idea. Ask around and see if someone can direct you in the right direction, look online, reach out to people that you admire in your industry. You will be surprised, there are people out there who would love to help a budding entrepreneur. You may have to invest in some coaching but with the right coach your investment will be worth way more than what you invested!

Want to work with me? Log on to
www.IamShannonAnderson.com
to find out more about me and my programs.

Identity

Your image is half the battle. The way that you see yourself determines what you will receive and what you will get out of life. You see, if you don't feel that you deserve something, you will never attract it. Will you even do what it takes to achieve it? If you don't believe that you deserve a million dollar home, will you ever do what it takes to have it? Will you go after the career or business that is required to obtain it? Will you call the real estate agent and ask her to take you on a tour to view the best homes in that million dollar price range so that you can visualize?

The answer is likely no. You see even if you don't believe in the law of attraction, which is the law of attracting the things that we want. If you don't believe that you deserve it, you will never even take the actions necessary to have them anyway. See how that works?

So let's do some exercises to level up our identity.

"Let's see ourselves bigger and greater than what we currently are so that we can become the best we've ever been."

Close your eyes and imagine the highest version of yourself.
What are you doing?
Where are you?
What are you wearing?

_____

_____

_____

_____

On the best day of your life, write out the activities that you are doing from the time that you wake up until the time that you go to bed.

_____

_____

_____

_____

Remember, there are no limitations! Write this exercise out as if you already have everything that you need to accomplish it.

Write it out here:

_____

_____

_____

_____

Powerful people read!

What books have you read lately(besides this one :)?

Reading is truly fundamental. All of the great leaders and thought leaders of the world read. That is not a coincidence. Studies have shown that people who read are far more successful than people who don't.

The difference between highly successful people and those who aren't is simply knowledge. Also reading keeps your mind sharp and ready for whatever!

P.S Also many highly successful people don't just read, they also write books as well! Are you ready to write your book? Log on to www.WriteAndPublishIn90Days.com to find out how you can get on track to writing your book!

What books can you read to elevate your life?

_____

_____

_____

What books do you already have that you haven't gotten around to that you can start reading today?

_____

_____

_____

Don't Be Dope, Broke, And Fabulous

Budget

Set A Budget: So let's start off with setting a budget. I have provided one below to start with. First we want to start off by adding up ALL of your income. That includes child support, side hustles, or any other sources that you can think of.

Next we want to deduct our expenses. The total that's left is what you have to work with.

Key: Let's see if we can deduct and lower bills, interest rates, cut out some of our entertainment, etc.

How much income do you make monthly?

What are your monthly expenses?

Monthly Income Total:					
Car Note					
Insurance					
Groceries					
Daycare					
Utilities					
Credit Cards Entertainm ent					
Hair					
Nails					
Miscellane ous					
Loans					
Total After Expenses:					

Invest

Now it's easier than ever to invest. Whether that's through day trading, stock trading, and or real estate. The goal is to take your money and flip it as much as you can.

Here I have listed a few apps and service providers that you can use to start your investing journey.

Key: It's good to start investing into companies that you know and use.

Acorns: Acorns is an easy app to use to start investing. I like the fact that they have a great option called Later where you can start your Roth IRA. It also gives you the option to do round up, which is where you can round up all of your purchases to the nearest dollar and Acorns will invest that money for your future!

Digit: A great way to save, it allows you to also round up and save money on your behalf.

Robinhood: *A really easy way to get into investing into stocks. Robinhood has a really easy interface to use and is pretty straight forward. You can easily go into the search and put in your favorite companies. Robinhood also allows you to invest into crypto currencies.*

A great resource for purchasing real estate is a site called Auction.com. Being able to get a list of foreclosures and pre foreclosures in your city is a great way to start investing into real estate. Also, reach out to some good real estate agents in your area to assist you with your search. Contact your county tax commissioner and ask how to get a hold of their tax lien auctions' list and sale.

Save

Being able to save for a rainy day and unforeseen circumstances is highly important. We never know what tomorrow holds, so it's great to be able to be prepared.

Goal: At least 3 months of all your expenses saved in an untouched saving's account

Digit: A great way to save, it allows you to also round up and save money on your behalf.

Acorn: Allows you to round up and save as well as invest in your Roth IRA for the future. It also allows you to take as low as $5 per week, month, or whatever time you set and will withdraw it automatically to reach your saving goals. Acorn also gives you a debit card.

You can also go the old fashioned route. If using cash, whenever you break a $100 dollar bill, save all of the 10's, and 20's. If you break a $20dollar bill, save all of the 5 dollar bills and so on...

MENTOR ME PLEASE

*So many people have asked me,
Shannon, how did you become the
woman that you are today? How did you
go through so many hardships, yet still
manage to become a best selling author,
build a successful publishing and
coaching company, turn your book into a
film while licensing it to Amazon, TubiTV,
and other networks? Yes, it took a lot of
work, faith, belief in myself as well as
coaching and mentorship. They say that
there is no elevator to success, only
stairs. Yet, I say that if you want to run
up the steps faster, get someone who's
been where you're trying to go to teach
you.That is truly where my life changed.
Once I invested in myself and found
people to teach me, that is when I got
unstuck, stopped hitting walls and leveled
up!*

Who do you look up to and why?_____

_____

Who can you reach out to mentor or coach you to your next level?

_____

Why would you select them?

_____

____

"I get what I want. If I don't have it then it's on its way"

"Speak what you seek until you see what you've said"

.

Thank you so much for reading The Glow Up! I hope that this book helps you in your journey to pursuing bigger and better things. Look at it as your bible on glowing up and getting what you want out of life. Refer back to it often whenever you need a boost!

Please follow me on Instagram at:
www.Instagram.com/IamShannonAnderson
www.Facebook.com/IamShannonAnderson

Resources

Publish Your Book

Www.PopPublishing.com

Want more resources?

Go to www.IamShannonAnderson.com to check in with the latest news

Ready to write your own book? Go to www.WriteAndPublishIn90Days.com and check out the free training

www.ingramcontent.com/pod-product-compliance
Lightning Source LLC
LaVergne TN
LVHW051809080426

835513LV00017B/1882